Burnt Offerings

Poems on Crime and Punishment

For Jada,

Robert Johnson

Robert Johnson

BleakHouse Publishing
New York

2007

Burnt Offerings

Poems on Crime and Punishment

By

Robert Johnson

With Poems by

Ania Dobrzanska

Seri Palla Irazola

Thaïs H. Miller

Cover Art:
Jennifer Adger

Cover Design:
Amy Hendrick
Jason Diebler

Copyright © 2007 by Robert Johnson

ISBN-13:   978-0-9797065-0-9
ISBN-10:   *0-9797065-0-5*

BleakHouse Publishing   *BHP*
(*bleakhousepublishing@gmail.com*)
67 Wall Street
22nd Floor, #8104
New York, NY 10005-3111

For my wife, Deirdra McLaughlin, whose humane sensibilities inform my life and my work.

Acknowledgments

Some of the poems in this collection have appeared in the following publications, to whose editors grateful acknowledgment is made: *Tacenda Literary Magazine*, *CMC* (Crime Media Culture), *Dan River Anthology*, and an earlier collection of my poems (*Poetic Justice*) published by Northwoods Press, a division of the Conservatory of American Letters.

I thank Thaïs H. Miller for reading and rereading my poems with a keen eye for detail and a superb ear for sound, and of course for the wonderful poem she contributed to this volume. My thanks are also extended to Ania Dobrzanksa and Seri P. Irazola for the moving poems they contributed to the book. The hard work and generous sentiments expressed by Charles Huckelbury (Foreword), Erin George (Reflections) and Susan Nagelsen (Afterword) are greatly appreciated. The book is much better for their efforts.

Other Books by Robert Johnson

Social Science
Culture and Crisis in Confinement

Condemned to Die

Hard Time

Death Work

Edited Volumes
The Pains of Imprisonment

Crime and Punishment

A Life for a Life

Life without Parole

Fiction
The Crying Wall

Justice Follies

Poetry
Poetic Justice

Sunset Sonata

Contents

Foreword

One of the most common fallacies that attend a prison sentence is the idea that only those of us actually doing the time can write adequately about it. That is, prose or poetry treating the prison experience must come from an incarcerated writer to be valid, for example, Oscar Wilde's poignant description of his imprisonment in "The Ballad of Reading Gaol" (1898). By this parochial standard, however, one would have to discount literary gems such as *The Count of Monte Cristo* (1844), simply because, although he wrote persuasively about betrayal and prison, Dumas père never saw the inside of a cell. Clearly something is amiss, deriving from the naïve supposition that only we on the inside suffer, and thus only we are qualified to describe that suffering.

Contrary to this solipsistic misconception, poetry is not the exclusive domain of individuals in a particular environment at any specific time. Indeed, inspiration for improbable subjects can knock at unexpected moments in unlikely places, since, as Coleridge[1] perceptively observed, "all good poetry is the spontaneous overflow of powerful feelings." Those powerful feelings are circumscribed by neither place nor time but are recognized by the contemplative mind that then produces a poetic response.

On the other side of the equation, good poetry requires participation by a reader capable of an empathetic response, because it is about the human experience, both transcendent and existential. Thus, when it comes to describing the phenomenon of imprisonment through verse, the poets inside share more than most of us are willing to admit with the poets on the outside, who, since they are removed from the devastation itself, often bring a fresher and more nuanced perspective to the task of conveying that destruction to an inexperienced reader.

This is Robert Johnson's accomplishment in his collection of poems, and he goes about his art by taking his readers on an

---

[1] Wordsworth usually gets the credit for this comment, for no other reason than he wrote the preface to Lyrical Ballads (1798), but most scholars agree that, since Coleridge was the superior literary critic, the definition is his.

elegiac journey from crime to arrest to confession to trial and ultimately to prison. The book is startling for both its poetic fluency and its stark accuracy, touching on themes unimaginable for the inexperienced, from the commercialization of the prison enterprise to the predatory practices of the cons doing the time and, along the way, unexpectedly but effectively incorporating musical inspiration from Paul Simon to Tommy Roe and the Bee Gees. The poetry exposes the myth of presumed innocence, as well as the institutionalized violence, by both guard and prisoner, that haunts prisons and points out the pernicious expansion of the prison mentality into society, including the public schools. Such arcane themes belong primarily to the men and women inside America's prisons, but Robert Johnson appropriates them and offers enlightenment to a wider audience in terms at once accessible to the general reader and acknowledged by few outside the system.

He fearlessly describes, for example, the ethical paradox of imprisonment and execution and their support by religious fundamentalists, and his psychological insights equal those of the most introspective prisoners: "Who we are... shapes what we see" ("I Witness"); "where color is life's prism" ("Our Black Prison Nation"); and, with a nod to Descartes, "I bleed, therefore I am" ("Desperately seeking freedom").

This collection is not, however, a Malthusian treatise on population control. In Johnson's poems, personal responsibility is inescapable, and the consequences are both immediate and far reaching. One of the most powerful pieces is "A Bend in the Road to Justice," a trenchant and harrowing description of both killer and victims in a murder trial, a perspective most of us inside would rather avoid but one which Johnson insists on putting before us. This is the poet at his persuasive best, precisely because of his ability to see and depict both sides simultaneously.

The most effective poets, free of self-imposed limitations, perceive the universals that unite us. Robert Johnson's poetry fulfills this aesthetic obligation by using prison as an intense, personalized, thematic vehicle but without avoiding the undeniable connection between the events inside prison and the philosophies that drive them on the outside. As Johnson puts it in his compelling closing poem, "What prisoners live, citizens dream / What citizens live, prisoners dream"

("Dreamscape"). There is, he reminds us, always this "intersection of civilization and chaos," one he urges us to negotiate very carefully.

William Carlos Williams[2] once observed that "It is difficult / to get the news from poems / yet men die miserably every day / for lack / of what is found there." In a world enervated by war and sadly lacking in empathy and understanding, Robert Johnson's collection of poems is an excellent alternative to that kind of premature and anguished death.

Charles Huckelbury, #19320
State Prison for Men
Concord, New Hampshire
10 April 2007

---

[2] "Asphodel, That Greeny Flower"

A Gun to the Head

A gun to the head,
a religious rite
in the Church of Crime,
Leaves a smudge
the size of a bullet hole

Robbers in black,
heads hooded
guns drawn,
make collection

"Gimme what you got, man.
It's for a good cause –
Cause I said so."

That's what they might say in the movies.
In real life, they sidle up next to your son
on a dark street, no one else around
Flash the gun, say "Understand?"
Then, "On your knees!"

Supplicant, eager to appease,
head bowed, digs deep
praying for release
moving as if in sleep
by rote, taking note
of crazy facts,
like the cracks
in the sidewalk,
moving, growing,
now wide enough
to swallow him whole

Delivered, if he is blessed with luck,
this side of heaven's shore,
of worldly goods and nothing more

"Is that all you fuckin' got!"
"Yeah, that's it"
"That's it!?
You just searched me, he thinks,
oddly detached, saying nothing,
as they run off into the night
leaving him alive, somehow, alright.

And the universe, blind, stumbles on
As if nothing at all were wrong
Dad out for an evening's walk
Mom visiting down the block
Brother shooting hoops by the light of the porch
Girlfriend (now wife) waiting for the nightly talk…

Everyone that matters
lost in mundane matters
while the planet had just now
spun on its axis, turned its celestial prow
moved one rotation faster
a hair's breath from disaster

Nuns with Guns

Nuns with guns
under their Habits
The next NRA gambit?

Already, we've got
God-Fearing, Man-Fearing
All-American Women
trained to shoot from the heel,
even the stiletto heel
(for dressy occasions)

Why not let nun's draw a bead?
Shoot to heal?
Wound to mend?
Kill to save?

Sister of the Gun
The Ultimate Nun
An Ultimatum of One

Say your prayers and
pass the ammunition
Save souls
shooting holes
in the body of crime

Christ Jesus Amen,
Will it ever end?

I Witness

An eye witness
is really an I witness.

Who we are, how we feel
shapes what we see.
Who we become
shapes what we saw

This see-saw is a
balancing act beyond
any scale of justice

Yet when we say,
"He's the one"
Our pointed finger's
As deadly as a gun

An Addict's Lament

Heroin's his heroine
long, languorous, a loyal followin'

Cocaine's her flame
burns high, hot, never tame

Crack everyone's whore
like a street walker, an easy score

Addiction's the action
ecstasy the traction
Where the chemical meets the road
helps you carry your load

Live for the high
Enough to get by
Life on the fly

Drug's the main man
no care, no plan
Kill the pain,
do it again

High's your niche
let's you scratch that itch
Bleeds the strife out of you
Bleeds the life out of you

A shoot up
A shoot out
Death the only route out.

Deadly

Needle, dart
Bull's-eye
Right to the heart

Gun, lead
Deadeye
Right to the head

Sad refrain
Never again

Sole shot
Soul shot

One less
To think about

Dope

Coke crazy
reefer lazy
life hazy

An existential fog

Sadness sprouts
like wild weeds,
so much burning brush,
hope gone up in
smoke

That's why they call it
dope.

overdose

living ghost
friends past
lives fleeting
moving fast
head in flight
speed of light

even when you fly
right
you just can't get
right
without another high
right?

living ghost
friends past
lives cast
moving fast
head in flight
speed of light

big vein
speeding train
right to the brain

good buy
goodbye

Name Game

They bought your drugs
You sold your life
They made you an offer
you couldn't refuse
though all you do is lose.
Now you're facing

Five to ten
Ten to life
Life with an out
Life without
Death on a gurney
the ultimate clout

The ball's in your court
to your own self be true
Rat someone out
get less time to do.
Guilty or not,
Most any name will do

Five to ten
Ten to life
Life with an out
Life without
Death on a gurney
the ultimate clout

They all play the same game
the criminal name game
cops and thugs in the same frame
That's how we fill our prisons
one rat at a time,
on each side of line.

Freudian Streets

pimps in pressed pampers
whores in dirty drawers,
johns looking for love

in all the wrong places
in orifices and faces
so many false traces
of care, seeds of

repressed desire, passion, fire
smoldering subterranean sublimation
driving this sordid underground nation
policed by cops with super egos and twisted notions
backed by rouge-red clubs and dark-black subterfuge
denial, unconsciousness the only refuge

Young thugs

Gun-toting toddlers
Fresh from mean cribs
Got dibs on survival

Take your candy
In a New York minute.

Ageless

If he can pull the
Trigger
He must be a
Bigger, Bolder, Older
Badass
than he looks

The First Time I Saw That Place
Thaïs *H. Miller*

"Up at the right there,"
"There above my right?"
"Right car mirror, there—
There's Juvie"
My driving instructor points out to me.

"Oh," I say, watching the cinder blocks rise
Rise up above the deserted hill, over
Over ramps of the freeway. Freeway.
Way to freedom, I know now, instinctively.
"In this world," he says, "there are only criminals and victims"

"The criminals go right."
Right to jail.
Right people turn left
"Left turn to merge onto the 101,
The freeway, towards home"
Home away from where we put...
Store, exile, hide away
Children who went wrong and now turn right,
Away from what "we want our children to see"

Seem like children to me,
Children we don't want to see.

A Patriarch's Protocol

Our Father
Who art in Headquarters
Hollow be Thy Claim
Thy Fortune Come
Thy Will be Mum
On CNN
and before
Congress.
Lead us Not
Into our Prison Nation
And Deliver us
From Civil Obligation
to our Fellow Man
Amen

School House Lockdown

When did we decide that public schools were prisons,
the kinds of places that sported metal detectors, cops,
locks on every door?

Was it when we decided that separate could not be equal?
Or when we decided we were not equal to the task of
educating the whole public, rich and poor, black and white, all
together?

Did we abandon public schools when they had to be public
schools rather than private schools run at public expense?

Our prisons are more repressive every day
Our schools are more prison-like everyday

Freedom?
Just another word for nothing left to lose?
Janis?
Janus?
Shame on us

Word Play

Deer
Game
Kill
Sport

Dear
Game
Kill
Spat

Assault Rifle
Sport
Hand Gun
Spat

Euphemism
Cynicism
Recidivism

Domestic Violence
Word

The Angry Marshal
By Seri P. Irazola

I had few expectations about the treatment of offenders prior to beginning my internship in September of 2003... On the second day of my internship... the defendants were shuffled out of the lockup cell and into a more crammed and uncomfortable cell behind the courtroom. I was sent to get one final interview. With few exceptions, access to this cell area is restricted to marshals and defendants. As an intern, I was not expected behind those doors. Standing back, clenching my clipboard, I watched in horror as an angry marshal started his daily speech to the defendants:

> "Listen up you *motherfucking* cocksuckers! You *stupid* pieces of dog shit! Hey! You *nigger* over there on the shitter...you best be paying attention to me too! Okay assholes, you *are* going to stand here as quiet as can be, and when I call your lockup numbers, you *are* going to walk forward. You *are* going to follow me into court, and you *are* going to stand there and lick that judge's ass as if she was your girl! If *any* of you decide that you are going to play tough, I will bring you back here and *not only* will I kick the living shit out of you, but I will put you into a cell without windows—where no one can hear you cry, and I promise you that an angry bunch of Marshals will come in there and make you wish you were never born! If you are going to go to jail tonight, and you know this, then take it like a man! We need to get through this quick! No one in here wants you to be fucking it up, because *all* you *motherfuckers* have to be seen today! My old lady has dinner on the table at 5:00pm every fucking night. If any of you act up, and I have to stay here to deal with you, my lady is gonna kick my ass, and that means that I am going to have to stay here extra long to pull my boot out of your ass for pissing off my lady! Now, not a fucking word out of you fuckers! Number 4, 78, and 89, step up *now*!

Presumption Gumption

We find no atheists on the battlefield
Where death looms
Nor innocents in the court room
Where convictions bloom

Guilt, that's the presumption
Though we lack the gumption
To admit it straight out.

By the time you get to Court,
No one thinks you're innocent.
No one. Not really, anyway.
Even your mother has her doubts.

You're dirty, manhandled from day one,
Greasy prints and donut crumbs all over you.
Pushed around, head bent
Kept at arm's length
Cruisin' for a bruisin'
Down for the count.

Cops sniff you out,
paw you around
leave you dazed and numb,
ready for the DAs
the big cats these days,
who direct your sorry ass
to court that fateful day
your corpus (read carcass)
dragged and gagged
(sometimes literally)
before a judge
on high
a robed figure with a big gavel,
an ancient artifact,
polished but pointless
since His Honor is flanked

by officers with modern guns
and presides over a silent line
of humbled humanity,
fresh from cramped cages,
Unkempt, unrested, uneasy
even queasy
Compliant to a fault

They've been prepped
Marshals know where they live

The judge calls all the shots
Bang, Bang
Order in the Court!
By Order of the Most Honorable Court!
Everyone else goes through the motions
when you get right down to it,
Following his script

"All Rise," shouts the Bailiff,
Often old and thin,
He might as well say,
"Let the Battle Begin"
and under his breath,
"We're eager to fight
'cause we almost always win."

You, hunched down,
Under a cloud of suspicion,
On the defensive, not called
defendant for nothing,
Relying for your freedom
maybe your life
On a Defense Attorney,
A Public Defender, most often,
Guardian of the poor public,
Green folk who fend off, as best they can,
the formidable forces of justice,
secure in the deep pockets of Uncle Sam

15

This is a trial alright, a crucible, a test,
featuring, if you raise your hand
and take the stand,
a cross examination – you,
At the left hand of the father
clearly on the outs,
Hammered by the prosecutor
questioned coldly, crossly
Handled crossly, coldly
fixed in place
for all to see.

Your life an open book,
suspended, spread-eagled
exposed

People figure, "God knows,
We'd never crucify an innocent man"

It started at the beginning,
when you talked to the detective
"Just tell your story," his gentle directive,
like he wants to hear a bedtime tale
after a long day putting people in jail.
But he didn't say, "It will be lights out for you,"
when he offered soft drinks, coffee, gum to chew.
Snack-and-chat hour though
he served the DA none other than you.

Hungrily, she ground your words,
Now called a confession, into nugget-sized
lumps of culpability, easily digested,
fast food for judge and jury
Who select a sentence
From a list of approved options

Read carefully, as
The menu has changed.

Settling on an American Standard:
Shake, bake, and serve time.
Easy as apple pie

Court is a world of words.
Words rule, talk counts.
"I withdraw the question,"
an attorney might say
Puff, it's gone.
"Ignore that comment."
Voila. Never happened!
"The jury is to disregard..."
the judge intones,
in basso falsetto.
Disregard what?
A bell that rang?
The latest harangue?
The whole panoply of power
paraded before them?

It's like magic,
Black Magic,
engrossing
even entertaining
in a dark way,
A juridical Disney Land
a modern wonder
Unless you're the one
Nailed on cross,
Desperately seeking
Redemption.

Sentence Gridlock

He tried to scale the wall, scrambling for a toe-hold
in the formidable edifice of federal sentencing rules
Rock solid, brought to an angry public
by an over-wrought Congress.

He'd been warned,
it's treacherous stuff, a long fall.

People pay for hard justice
in our Donation Nation
Go soft, soft money's
hard to come by.

Digging in,
getting a good grip
He began to chip
away, case by case,
relying on pertinent facts,
sharply on point

Knocking time off here
tacking on a program there,
Depending
on things like
The person, The crime, The particulars.

Controversial
these days
Days of the
Justice Infomercial

*Get the latest and greatest sentencing kit
One sentence fits all, Satisfaction guaranteed
But wait, there's more...*

Got his hands slapped, told
Justice is a board game

like chutes and ladders
Where you fall
tells it all

Do the crime
get the time
No gray
least not today

Tomorrow?
who can say
Supreme Irony
ever at play

Zero tolerance

Zero tolerance
Zero commonsense

I'm a pro
Don't need to know

Context?
Complex!

It's the rule,
It's the law,
Don't tell me more

Demons One and All

At the bar of justice
Innocence is no bar to
Conviction
Confinement
Condemnation
Consignment
to the junkyard of lost souls.

After the fall
we brand criminals
Demons
One and all
Once and for all

Innocent? Too late,
too good to be true
A technicality, not fate
not the real you.

We swallow our mistakes,
keep them safe and warm
In the belly of the beast
where they belong.

Go Straight

Go straight
to your date
with
Poverty
Homelessness
Joblessness
Hopelessness

Go straight
to jail
Do not pass Go
Do not collect 200 dollars
Do not land on Public Housing

Go straight
back home
Where lepers roam
scarred, marred
tattooed, screwed
Folk like you

The Underclass
The Déclassé
Folk we throw away

Pod People

Human husks wrapped in scorn
solitary figures, mute, forlorn
lay flat, unmoving, unmourned
arms crossed, faces slack
eyes half open, glazed, black
tortured on a modern rack

Buzzers beep, hum, a morning rite
inert figures come to life
a marionette review,
run in mime, lost in time

Over go pairs of feet,
thwack, thwack,
flat on the floor
Slowly rises each torso,
twisting, creaking,
turning gingerly toward the door
Carefully moves each form,
dragging, shuffling,
inching toward the murky light
Sepia-toned, heavy,
etched in grime, thick with blight
detritus of a long dark night

Each man, each day, in his way
goes the distance, makes his bones
traversing his cloistered world alone
touring his cell, his private hell
dancing with his demons
dreaming he's a free man

All this, yet no one knows
no one heeds these one-man shows
one puppet per stage, one prisoner per pod
one guard, on guard
unseeing, unseen

runs the supermax machine
a padded vest, hands gloved in gray
pushes buttons, shoves trays
recedes, a phantom, into the haze

People of the Pod,
pomanders and epithets
pressed to sweaty chests like amulets,
breathe deeply of the fetid air,
speak daily to God, Care
only that He use the Rod

"Punish me," they say, "for I am bad"
His Word redounds,
comes off the wall, off the page,
floats in space, feeds their rage
each cell a terminal stage
a killing cage, for men

stoned, dazed, left to fate
blinded by a bright white hate,
wallowing in delusion
stewing in corruption
yearning for direction,
to be a Somebody
not just some body

Solitary Soliloquy
By Ania Dobrzanska

I hear music no one else hears. I see things no one else sees. In a cell alone, I have a whole world before me. In the hole, I am swallowed whole, tortured and tormented, torn apart.

Fear washes over me, cold and close, numbing my limbs, paralyzing my thoughts. Each second a snapshot, exposed, explored, stretched... I feel. I feel a drop of sweat trickle down my pale face. Blood rushes through my veins, pounding in my chest, ringing in my ears; my muscles tense, then cramp. Parched throat like a sandy dessert, thirsty, hungry, exhausted...I've exhausted all senses, now I'm numb. It is me against the world and I am not ready.

I sense them outside my door, lurking. The creaking of steel doors, slow and low, tells me I am at the gates of hell, two devils in military gear my unlikely escort. Like an enormous wave on a raging sea, freezing cold crashes against me, drowning my heartbeat, blurring my vision, stealing my breath.... raping me, leaving me empty, shivering, unmoving, jammed between two worlds, the living... and the dead. Trapped, wedged between terror and rage, I want to fight but I see it, the darkness of the hole, the pit, waiting for me, drawing me down, sucking the life out of me in an instant. I relent.

The hole lives, that I know. I'm scared... I scream, but no one hears. I cry, but no one sees. I hear nothing. I see nothing. I am here but I am gone. I am inside myself, and inside the hole. I am the hole, and the hole is me.

Will I ever be free?

Colossal Corrections Clearance Sale

Starts Today! 3 Great Ways to
Save, Save, Save
On that Prison Cell we've earmarked for you!

This is the Real Deal,
The Big Deal.
The Colossal Corrections Clearance Sale!

Huge selection of models
Singles, doubles, and more
Some with a view
All color coordinated
Bars included
On Terms that are a
STEAL

Plus, our SUPER Rewards Special
Up to half off on Early Bird selections
An extra 15% off with Bonus Coupons

Regular Offenders get a 10% Reward Card

Get-out-of-jail- free cards **not** accepted with this offer!

The Big Hurt

Death by automation
Pain by remote control
Distant, impersonal
Machine-tooled, Factory-fresh
Mechanized Executions

Reliable
Guaranteed
Check warranty for details

Here's how it works:
A conveyor belt
run to death row
ferries flaccid felons
carb-fed, half-dead
plucked, shucked,
routed on ramps
everyone amped.

Featuring our Patented,
No-Touch System:
Loading Robots (L-Bots)
Place Package (Offender) on belt,
Receiving Robots (R-Bots)
accept, transfer Package to
Terminal Robots (T-Bots),
ever-ready, ever-revved
Programmed in mega-hertz
to deliver the Big Hurt
On demand.

Assembly-line slaughter
something to see
Robots L, R & T --
better than TV

Some assembly required
Powers down automatically
Stores well

burnt offerings

there
in the damp basement
of the aging prison
near the
chair

death
the scent of
burnt offerings
hangs in the
air

a
devil's brew of
mildew, flesh, and
fear

the
chair is gone
(the latest reform)
the smell lives
on

Last supper

A fried steak, diced into little squares,
arrives at the death house,
neatly reassembled, like a puzzle,
laid to rest in the center berth
of a standard white Styrofoam box,
bordered on one side by soggy, sagging fries,
on the other by wilted greens, curled and brown,
long past their salad days, like the man himself,
who ordered this meal as the sad celebration,
culmination, of a dreary, wasted life
that it is even now slipping away,
as he ages before our eyes right there in his cell,
called "the last night cell" in some prisons,
"the death cell" in this one.

Later, he will be cooked, in a manner of speaking,
in the electric chair, but not diced or reassembled,
before he is boxed without frills in a plywood coffin,
the mortuary's answer to the Styrofoam box, and
buried in the prison cemetery, home to the
most common and indigestible waste
of the prison system.

He eats alone with a plastic fork –
no knives for the condemned,
no dinner companions for the condemned –
chewing carefully, kneeling by his bed, as if in
genuflection before the raw power of the state,
his meager meal placed carefully on the steel gray metal bed,
sitting precariously on the top sheet, drawn tight
like a sail battened down for heavy weather.

We look at each other tentatively, almost furtively,
lawyers, chaplains, even officers speaking in low tones,
words directed toward the ground,
as if we are greasy, dirty, our mouths dry,
tongues swollen, sticking to our teeth,

our noses stinging from the scent of corruption,
the bittersweet stink of fear in the air
in our hair, on our skin, in our clothes.

We are guests at a living wake
where the dead live,
where the dead see,
look you in the eye and see nothing,
see no one will save them
see they are utterly alone.

The condemned man finishes his meal,
says 'thank you' to the officers who fed him dinner,
then walks with them to his execution, on schedule,
dead before the stroke of midnight. We go home,
stomachs empty, hungry for sleep.

Notes from Planet Prison

"Inmate attends church weakly," it was noted in the file. The
fight was serious, we learn in an entry from another file, since
the man "went for the juggler vein." Another fight was ruled
"a clear-cut case of elf defense." An inmate was punished for
"making a para-military jester," which may be a comedian in
camouflage, a distant relative of the juggler noted above, or at
least someone on good terms with prison elves.

No Vacancies Allowed

You may be innocent
But you won't get one cent
From some jurisdictions
Where predilections
Favor punishment
For its own sake
Like we have a stake
In the Big House.

No Vacancies Allowed
Say it loud
Say it proud

Prison Business

The Business of Prisons
Is Business

Profits first
With all due
Consideration

To money
Honey
And little
Else.

Our Black Prison Nation

At first blush, today's black prisons
look like a green wound, a fresh assault,
something new under the sun.

But Old Hannah* burns hot and relentless
on peoples pushed to the margins,
exposed, defenseless.

This modern conflagration is but a recapitulation
of patterns dating back to our country's creation
seen all too clearly in slave ship and plantation
in share cropper hut and urban underclass station
reaching full flower in our black prison nation.

A world apart, so black, so rife with misery
the prison is utterly foreign to those who be
wealthy, especially white and wealthy,
those paragons of privilege given a healthy
dose of justice in the land of the free

So it is, as ever, a given:
The rich get richer
and the poor get prison.
Especially in the slums
where color is life's prism.

A lucky few from penal interment
come risen (after three decades, not three days)
but they, unlike Christ
are unbidden
and unwelcome
in the land where only
the white
and wealthy
are truly free.

*Note: Old Hannah is a name for the sun found in slave and plantation prison songs.

31

Mister Rogers Prison

It's a beautiful day in the prison
Yard
But none of us can go too
Far
So could ya',
would ya'
Be
my cellmate?

Oh, sure, I know.
Cellmate.
That's a cold name.
Nobody wants to be called
Cellmate.
It's Cell Buddy,*
Isn't that right?
OK, be my Cell Buddy?
Thanks.
I'll be your Cell Buddy, too!

Welcome to Mister Rogers Prison.
A Special place for
Special boys and girls,
Bad boys and girls,
Mostly bad boys

Here's a bad boy now,
Walking down the tier.
Hey, there, Butch, love the tattoos.
What does that one say?
"Go Fuck yourself!"
Oh, my. Well, it's a free country, isn't it?

Ah, Just a figure of speech, Butch.
I know you're not free here, not really.
No offense intended…
Sure, I can mind my own fucking business.

Let's see who else is around today.
Hey, Juan. There's Juan, coming out of his cage.
We call cages home here, kids.
Snappy shank, Juan. Makes a statement.
Great what you've done with duct tape.
There are so many uses for duct tape
In prison and on the outside, too.

Did you know that Bubba?
Bubba looks like he's in a coma
He just wandered up to us, looking confused.
Bubba's got an imaginary Cell Buddy
Tells Bubba what to do
No trouble from Bubba.
Just stay on your meds, Bubba,
You'll be fine.

Mister Rogers Prison is a Diverse Place
We've got Rough boys, Tough boys, Gruff boys
Boys who can't play well with others.

We've got boys who like little boys
A lot.
A whole lot
Maybe a whole lot too much

Lawrence, let little Ricky off your lap.
Ricky's doing life but he looks about ten years old.
Ricky's squirming, Lawrence, he wants to get down.
You like the squirming?
Well aren't you the patient one?
Isn't he patient, Ricky?
Ricky?
Oh, OK, no problem.
Somebody clean Ricky up.
No need to cry, Ricky.
These things happen.

We wish we had more girls
in Mister Rogers Prison,
Don't we Ricky?
But our boys would keep hurting them
And they'd tell Mr. Screw
And I guess you know what he'd do.
Yes, Mister Rogers Supermax Prison.
We can't even broadcast from there!

Well, that's enough for today.
Until tomorrow, remember
lock your cell
and run like hell
If you get a play date
That just doesn't feel right.

* Cell buddy is the term used for cell mate in Maryland prisons.

No-where Men

A prisoner is a
no-hole mouse   Behind
no-mercy walls   In
no-hope cages

He's got a
no-future life   In a
no-home world   With
no-where to go   But
hole-up in prison

Supersize My Prison, Please

Like to Supersize that prison, mister?

You betcha! Sounds keen!
Bigger, bleaker dungeons –
More punishment, more green.

Prisons, cheaper by the pack,
Prisoners, a bargain by the million.
Lock em up and don't look back.
Think of prison as an underclass cotillion.

Who said America didn't have balls?

Last night lullaby

Good night moon
Good night gloom
Good night uniform and plastic spoon
Good night keeper of this chilly tomb

Good night cell
Good night smell
Good night screams of man and bell
Good night tiers in this living hell

Good night tears that each night fell
Quietly, privately, on my pillow
Hidden from the other fellow
Struggling, too, with dreams gone fallow

Good night moon
Good night gloom
Good night to my metal cocoon
(too cold for me to call a womb)
Tomorrow brings release from pain
A new life ready to bloom again

50 ways to kill your convict

The problem's to get him dead, she said to me
The method is easy, if you take it one, two, three
I can help you in your work you'll soon agree
There must be fifty ways to kill your convict

You gotta stay cool, Yul
Do it after dark, Mark
Just follow the plan, Stan
And get the man dead

Go Cook 'em in a chair, Blair
Dose him on a gurney, Ernie
Choke him with a noose, Bruce
It all works for me

Get him on a stretcher, Fletcher
Drop him at the morgue, George
Put him in a grave, Dave
Then you're all done, Son
Just take it from me.

Adversary Justice

Adversary, enemy
Righteous authority
Subhuman entity
Formula for entropy

Justice grinds slowly
to a dead halt
Vengeance takes flight
on bloodied wings

All you convicts

All you convicts gather round
to hear a tale of great renown
of young boys raped and old men cowed
In golden days when convicts bowed
to no man
no where,
no how

and staff knew their place
and cons knew the score
and weak was just another word for whore
for folk who'd bend over backwards
to get out the door

Cell block serenade

Hey, Hey
he's my little Sheila
tattoos and a pony tail

Love a little fem
like my little Sheila
man that little con is fine
you know I got to make her mine

Hey, Hey
he's my little Sheila
her mane
drives me insane

Love a little fem
like my little Sheila
man that little trick is mine
even if her name is Ryan

Buried Alive

You can tell by the way I use my walk,
I'm a convict man, not 'bout to balk
Cell block's loud and women gone,
I've been kicked around
since I was born

And now it's all right, It's OK.
And you may look the other way
And you can try to understand
what doin' time does to a man.

Whether you're a drugger or whether you're a mugger
You're buried alive, buried alive.
Feel your life shakin', feel your heart breakin'
You're buried alive, buried alive
Ha, ha, ha, ha, buried alive, buried alive
Ha, ha, ha, ha, buried alive, buried alive

You can tell by the way I flash my tats
I'm hard-edged man, gotta give me that
My guns are strong and my rep is long
I've been kickin' butt since I was born

And now it's all right, It's OK.
And you may look the other way
And you can try to understand
what doin' time does to a man.

Whether you're a drugger or whether you're a mugger
You're buried alive, buried alive.
Feel your life shakin', feel your heart breakin'
You're buried alive, buried alive
Ha, ha, ha, ha, buried alive, buried alive
Ha, ha, ha, ha, buried alive, buried alive

Now I'm ready to walk right out that door
I've paid my debt, that's for sure
However you figure, I've evened the score
'cause prison is dying, prison is death
now I'm resurrected, get to draw fresh breath

Now it's all right, It's OK
I get to live another day
And you can try to understand
How bein' free feels to a man

Custom Framing

Convictions
made to order
Lineups
but no lines
Evidence
cut to specifications
Background
shaded to taste
Exotic
samples, models
Cuffed
buffed, ready to
Mount

Get orders in early
Beat the weekend rush

Repeat customer discounts available
Some jobs require extra time

A service of police predilections,
"Where the truth lies" and
"We stand on our convictions"

Gang Associate

They said he was a
"prison gang associate."
He felt proud
He'd come a long way
from gangsta, banger,
home boy from the 'hood.
He'd shown his wood.

"My associates and I
are gathered here on
this fine evening to
expropriate your funds
liquidate your assets
and generally
kick your ass."

That's how associates talk
as everyone knows
in and out of prisons

"Your cooperation
is deeply appreciated –
About six inches deep,
should you wish to know,
In your chest and neck.
if you tell us 'no'"

He takes a bow
then makes a vow

"So hand over the bling
let me do my thing
And you go home to mama
get to relive the drama"

He'll make partner one day soon
and maybe a cell with a view.

No Convict Left Behind

We don't leave students behind
No matter how troubled they may be
Why abandon convicts?
Folks once like you and me –
Before slum schools and savage inequity
Set them on a course of angry iniquity
Free of restraint, instruction, direction,
On a one-way street to destruction,
Theirs and ours.

If corrections can't correct,
Correct corrections.
If prisons don't reform,
We've ignored them too long.
Prisons have been around since forever
You'd think we had a lock on this endeavor.

A warehouse is no house of change
Just a junkyard for people and pain
(Theirs and ours.)
But prison could be a place of reflection
For the wayward, a route to resurrection.

Instead of the third degree
Give convicts a living degree
A grade for adjustment, A measure
of our setting, their vetting.
It's all a transaction
focus on the daily action.

Why not Honor the Honorable
With a Certificate of Correction
A Seal of Good Prison Living
A Stamp of Mature Coping
A Symbol of Growth in Adversity

Put them on a fast-track to a new life
Courtesy of a Concerned, Committed, Corrections
Community, Standing by its alumni.

Rehabilitation guaranteed
Defects remedied
Upon return

Why not Acknowledge the Adequate
With a Certificate of Completion
They've done their stretch,
Paid their debt
Set accounts right
Give them a second bite
At life.

Prospects good
Liberal repair,
Return policy

Why not Mark the Failures,
the mad
the bad
the terminally inept
all who need to be kept
under the gaze of authority
in prison and out
With an Incomplete, or better, an
In Progress Badge, for those
Not yet ready for primetime,
But reachable in due time,
Open to renovation
If we summon the energy,
muster the innovation.

Buyer beware
Emergency recall
Twenty-four, seven

Progress in Living
Our most important product
Some setbacks to be expected
Others certifiably corrected

Corrections Commencement Ceremony

"Survivor First Class Smith,
reporting for release, sir."
Smith stands erect, chest swelling,
Ready for the coveted C – Corrected,
to be pinned on his crisply pressed shirt

Call it the Gentleman's C
For those we hope to see
Out and about
Living a good life

"Survivor Second Class Rodriques,
reporting for release, sir."
Rodriques is awarded the enigmatic A – Acceptable,
For those we say
may one day
make their way
Our way

"Survivor Third Class Jones,
Ready to go."
"Isn't that, 'Ready to go, Sir?' asks the Warden.
"Ready to go, sir," replies Jones.

Awarded the hopeful IP – In Progress
Jones may one day be
Free, like you and me
To sail in life's rough lee
Stable, free
Amid the tempest of temptation, strife
That was his criminal life.

Our Tier

Our tier, our town, look around
cells and surround sound
petulance, flatulence, a tortured tune
Walls ain't coming down any time soon

But the world comes in
On radio and TV signals
Audible at any decibel
Crashing all around us
Drowning us

In a sea
We can't see
Not clearly
Not really

SHU Fly

Lifers lie dormant in prison cells
some in SHUs
that's Special Housing Units
pronounced Shoes
where prisoners are buried deep,
underground,
like cicadas
stored and ready for resurrection
some 17 years hence
(if they're lucky)

One day they wake up free;
startled, they stumble to life
hands over their eyes
flying blind
carcasses strewn everywhere

Florescent Lighting

The prison had standard fluorescent lighting,
little flourished there
under the harsh glare.

The tubes dispelled the darkness
but shed an unflattering light on life
Revealing scars and lesions
the occasional suppurating sore

Even smells seemed worse, somehow,
as if they radiated off dirty, sweaty bodies
Blinding you with an acrid haze,
Stink that stayed with you for days.

Let there be light!
said the Lord
Who never did time
in a modern prison

Let there be florescence!
that would be something.

Fluorescent lights may last for life, but
Florescence, well, that makes life worth living

Days of Our Lives
By Seri P. Palla

"Like sand through the hourglass"
that turned to mud and got stuck
I wait

In a concrete room
with grey walls and floors
and a steel bunk
I wait

On a bed that has held
so many bodies
other than my own
That has tasted semen, blood, tears
other than my own
I wait

For surcease
Release

Relief
from this life
Where sand turned to mud
And time stopped

These are the days of our lives
These are the days of my life

VIPs

Virtually Imprisoned Persons
Trapped in images
Drowning in slogans
Bleeding from sound-bites
Worried about their makeup
Not their constitution

Appearances count
Surfaces suffice

Superficiality
Beats technicality
Image
Beats substance
Pictures
Tame arguments
Belief
One good exposure
away

Don't complain or explain
Makes you look lame
Just smile
For the cameras.

Virtually Imprisoned Persons
Trapped in images
Living large
Living tame
Image and substance
One and the same

**What goes around, Or,
A sewer runs through it**

gray, gloomy stone wall
hulking, soaring

silver, shiny metal wire
sharp, gleaming

bare, barred steel cage
barren, bleeding

aluminum commode
cold comfort

flush
whoosh
discharge

They all
get out
They all
come back

Bringing
a little bit of prison
with them

Face it

Faces
Faces Framed
Faces Framed by steel cell bars
Faces Framed by stone and mortar walls
Faces Framed by leather-strapped gurneys
Faces Framed by plain box caskets
Faces Framed
Faces

Faces
Faces Framed
Faces Framed and Mounted
Faces of the Dead
Faces of Justice
Faces Framed
Faces

Box Canyon

Those crazy goons, thumping their chests, dancing in jerky motions, shoulders hunched, teeth bared, hootin' and hollerin', making a show of their show of force, telling the caged cons, "we're crazy motherfucka's, maybe as crazy as you, so come out the zoo, do what you got to do." Their prey wants to play, climbs the bars, shakes the cage, burns acrid black with rage, figures "fuckyou, I'm tired, I'm bored, I'm pissed, bring it on." Everybody wired, cold stoned on adrenaline, pumped, ready for a little corrective action. Hack and cons, locked in the box,* the hole, the end of the line, ready to get it on, doing time hard before hard time does them, moving to a beat as old as the wild and as new as a fresh wound.

* The box is slang for punitive segregation, a place of great pressure that gives way now and again to ugly confrontations between frustrated officers and inmates.

49

Mother's Milk of Amnesia

Mandatory time
Least we can do

Fight crime
Sacrifice a few

Toe the line
You'll be fine

A little slack
In your plan of attack?

Go back
To square one

Like nothing else matters
Since Day One

Mandatory Hell
Least we can do

Give you a cell
Reserved for two

You
And the horse you rode in on

Blessed Apartheid

Our Father
Keep us
Apart
From those we
Hate

Let them not
Dwell
Among us
Who are not
Just
Like us

Let the women
Be domestics
Domesticate
the men

Amen

Politics

We hate second thoughts
and the thoughtful people
who think them,
As if a mind can't be
changed
without being
short-changed

A Bend in the Road to Justice

A quiet moment
A break in the adversarial engagement
A young female attorney chats
Amiably with her client, a
Hulking man convicted of capital murder.
Beside them, nominally on duty,
A mustachioed guard, looking like a
genial refugee from the 1890s,
Smiles, nods, adds a light comment

Back a few rows and to their right, a
Lone woman, older, sustained
By a long thin oxygen tube, sits quietly,
deep in mourning for the victims
Both blood to her, both ripped from her life,
Both missed in a visible, visceral way.
She will be joined by family when court resumes,
And laughter will make quiet ripples in their grief,
Small escapes from the horror that has enveloped them.

They want justice and they may get it
But they'll get no relief, no reprieve,
From their life sentences, shadowed by death,
Lived one long day at a time.

A flickering light

A flickering light in a cell house window
licks the night-stained lime-stone wall,
violating the darkness
like a thief in the night,
stealing peace of mind
from the black hole
convicts call home

Two men lay within
on cement bunks
framed by bars
cast in shadows
minds in distant places
lost in races they hope one day to run

They read and dream by a solitary bulb
dangling from above
heads barely hidden beneath thinning hair
free for a time, maybe more free
than they will ever be

When prison gates close behind them
and they rejoin a world
barred to them
pretty much from the start.

Years of living alone

Years of living alone
leached the color from her face,
left her as pale as the concrete floor
she paced daily, nightly, ever so lightly
so as not to draw attention to herself
what was left of her self
barely visible
behind the bars
in the afterglow
of lights out
on death row

Don't let your babies grow up to be convicts

I aim to ride this day down into night
like a bronco that can't be tamed
to stay up 'til light, to put up a fight
against rules that say
lights out because it's time
wear a saddle, wear this brand
you're mine, doin' time

Plenty of time, alright
but no saddle in sight
no mark on my butt
so I stay up
reading
or just horsing around
looking for enlightenment
looking for a sign
looking for something that's mine
all mine

Old Men

The old men flaunt faded tattoos
that sing of boisterous youths
now fallen fallow on bony arms,
now heaving, rolling, on swollen guts
Daggers once held firm, at the ready,
hidden, wrapped in shrouds of fat
Guns, too, holstered in layers of flesh,
hard to reach
Names of mothers stretched
beyond recognition
Marriages celebrated, then broken
beyond repair
Men in decline,
serving time
Marked by life,
for life.

Desperately seeking freedom

O'er the cell a mark still lingers
Of where a convict's bloodied fingers
Could make stone speak of life's hard ends
With words that shine like darkling gems
I was here
I am a man
I bleed, therefore I am...
Alive, in a manner of speaking
It's raw, sweet freedom I'm desperately seeking
A prison cell's a coffin reeking
Of dreams gone sour
Of life died by the hour
Of death by decree
Until you're set free
In this life or the next

Asshole Buddies

"I remember the day,
when things went my way."

Both men nodded,
far off looks in their eyes,
nostalgia heavy in the air.

"When I'd say 'bend'
they'd say 'how far?'
When I'd say 'spread 'em'
they'd say 'how wide?'"

"Some of those guys, you
could see clear through their assholes
Right out their mouths!"

"Yeah, those were the days,"
sighed the aging ex-con,
no stranger to the backside of his fellow man,
warmed by reveries, nodding
toward the gray-haired guard
he'd known back in the days
when they did time for the state
behind the same gray walls,
inside the same gray world,
brighter now, somehow,
in hindsight.

Cell Mate
By Robert Johnson & Ania Dobrzanska

I sit before her, crouched
In the corner of our bare cell
Fully clothed, fully exposed,
Hurt, alone
Head shaking
Heart aching
Thoughts racing
I am a prisoner –
A prisoner of her rage
A prisoner in her cage
A prisoner of my own private death row
That's how things go
When abuse becomes a way of life
and death

She looms above me
An animal now with teeth bared
Words that bite, tear my flesh
I am a whore
I am a slut
I am trash
Unworthy, unwanted

She grows bigger with each insult
Swelling up, feeding off my pain
I shrink before her eyes
Dying a little inside

Later, she snuggles up to me
As if nothing had happened
"We'll get through this," she purrs.

We?

On the Yard

Muggers, rapists, robbers and thieves mill about aimlessly, or so it seems, among small-time junkies and dealers with big-time dreams, in occasional conferences, bargaining, overheard but not understood by the nut cases, men in their own orbit, on their own highs, in turn beset by the retarded, who think the crazies are conduits to the gods, think their hallucinations are harbingers of things to come, signs that hold answers to their muttered, stuttered pleas for guidance, direction, relief from the chaos that envelops their days and nights in the prison, a Playstation fantasy world where folks play for keeps and scripts get written and rewritten all the time.

Tattoos form a crazy quilt of sick art, rendered on human flesh, pointing the way to the various and sundry constellations on planet prison, one sadder or madder than the next. This way to gangs and girls (or a reasonable facsimile); that way to muscles with mothers perched on biceps; watch out for guns half hidden by boxer shorts, peeking out at the waist, as if in a holster; beware devils and goblins and serpents, medieval creatures loose on the sagging skin of bearded, ponderous, dangerous men, folk you watch out for, can't befriend.

Follow the yellow brick road but don't show yellow, fellow, or it's a long, long way from Kansas to where you'll be heading, a piece of meat, somebody's bedtime treat.

Primitive. Primeval. Just-plain-evil.

But there it is, there you are, far from home, trying to find a home on the prison range, where life is downright strange, and ain't nobody free.

Fishing

He baits his hook with
Snacks of all sorts
Cheese nibs
Chocolate chips
Gums and mints
And of course
Life Savers
Sweet Life Savers
In various flavors
Even Tropical Fruits
Hard to come by in this gray world

He hopes one of the young ones
Innocent and fair
(Relatively speaking)
Will nibble or bite
Or at least grab hold of him,
Reach for his outstretched hand
Grab on for dear life

For life can be dear
Even in prison
And utterly unbearable
Especially in prison
When you cast your reel
And the line comes back slack

Another chance at happiness
However sad or sordid,
That got away

A crown of thorns

A crown of thorns,
shiny, steel, serrated,
rests uneasily atop the walls of his world,
visible through thin windows carved from stone,
narrow slits that offer stunted slices of life
inside and out.

The prison, long and lean, modeled on a telephone pole,
looks like a makeshift crucifix in the dying light of day,
head and feet and hands festooned with towers,
now lit in backdrop, set off against the graying sky,
home to armed guards, guards

Who know not whom they may one day shoot
but know well there is no getting out of this inn
without Caesar's consent.

"Forgive them," he thinks, though these days
forgiveness is not for prisoners to give,
"Even if they know, all too well,
what they do."

Birthdays in the World

He walks across the dusty ground
hoary with frost so fine
the yard looks like
icing on an old cake;
brittle, broken up,
left over from birthdays
in the world, far from prison

Night Fright

He approaches the tawny, tattooed man
with tremulous, tentative steps
(his face a mask of stone)

It is twilight and the moon-soaked ground,
almost luminescent, threatens to give way,
to let him fall right out of this day
out of this place
out of this life

But the ground stands firm
and he stands firm
feet planted squarely
a shoulder's width apart

Gently he caresses his shank
(homemade, handmade)
to remind himself where he is
and what he is
and what he must do
to see another day

Postcards from Prison

The rocky road opens before him
then wraps around the quarry
from which the prison was built,
stone by stone
man by man
life by life
each piece of raw material
a wonder of nature,
the end result...
something less

Outside it's Christmas

Sheets of ice locked the prison down
like a deadbolt on a cell door,
everyone trapped inside
nowhere to go
the world still
time frozen
men cast in ice
cold as death

Outside it's Christmas
Inside it's Business

The New Year Approaches
The Old Year Reproaches

Prisoners and Keepers
As One
Stuck Dumb
By the sheer weight of time

Year Book

Head shots arrayed in columns and rows,
monuments to the harsh workings of time

Characters captured
fates sealed

In tears
on tiers

One life at a time
lost in time

He awakens

He awakens, drinks in the familiar stench,
notes the order of things in his cell –
steel commode, iron bars, cement walls –
feels the muggy warmth of sleeping men
Then breathes deep the raw wound of emptiness
and retreats into the soul-saving stupor of sleep
"Wake me when it's over," he thinks,
knowing the day will come too soon

Sign Language

"This door," the sign boldly proclaimed,
"is no longer a door."
There's little with words one can't do
Especially at Cambridge U
(where words are always given their due)
And so it was true
From henceforth to evermore
That door was no longer a door

Strange as it may seem
Others live by that dream

"This war," President Bush once proudly proclaimed,
"is no longer a war"
No longer, one supposes, a brutal whore
For bloody, ambitious, sordid vested interests
And misguided positions on key issues
Like, "they really want us there"
And, "you can tell we're winning when casualties mount
'cause frenzied killing is the last refuge of the desperate"
And, "democracy is just a torture chamber away"
(No one said that, in so many words
 but the pictures, that's another story)

Closer to home, we've heard it said:
"This prison is no longer a prison"
It is henceforth risen
From scorn, derision
Its unspoken mission
To become a correctional institution

"This slum," we've heard tell,
"is no longer a slum"
A world of massive dearth and meager mirth
Where folk work hard, die young
Unmourned, unsung
So much economic dung

"It's now a national park zone"
Where the wild animals roam
Unmolested
Unless they leave the
Reservation.

in which case we show them
the door

Dreamscape

Prisoners live like savages,
lost in the animal moment,
but secretly yearn for order
They are up on their toes,
alert but wary,
hungry for deep sleep

The rest of us are bruised daily
by the firm walls of convention,
and in our hidden hearts yearn
for the liberation of our senses,
for appetites sated, for moments
red and redolent of life lived raw

What prisoners live, citizens dream
What citizens live, prisoners dream

Prisons take root
at the intersection
of civilization and chaos

Cross with care

Reflections of A Woman and A Prisoner

I have to confess that I was shocked to receive a letter from Robert Johnson asking me if I were willing to share my thoughts on his collection of poetry. You see, I am an inmate at a women's correctional facility, and as such, I belong to a group that typically is disregarded (except that we are allocated scant, bitterly-begrudged dollars in the state budget).

Inmates often forget that there are people like Professor Johnson, who have explored the world of the incarcerated and found value there. What Johnson reveals in *Burnt Offerings* are not the flimsy stories of a sensationalized made-for-television movie, peopled by the shallow stereotypes so familiar from popular culture: the snitch, the gang leader, the effeminate homosexual, the muscle man (or woman), the token intellectual, and of course the innocent man who somehow (remember this is fiction) proves his innocence and returns home to weeping mother and steadfast spouse.

Most people won't want to see the reality glimpsed through these pages. Preferable is a tidy storyline all wrapped up within a neat two hours (including commercial breaks). The world Johnson recorded is not nearly that comfortable, but it is deeply real and it demands to be acknowledged.

Through his poetry, Johnson expresses the life borne by many entombed within the system. They cannot speak for themselves. Their experiences have silenced them. But like a surgeon, Johnson deftly exposes the sepsis that is the penal system of our ostensibly progressive society.

In uncovering the sad pattern of our being, Johnson casts an unrelenting light on a system that has institutionalized callousness and dehumanization. "Prison Business" and "Supersize My Prison, Please" show the true goal of our prison system—not rehabilitation, but running a lucrative business built on broken lives. The justice that Johnson reveals is based more on politics and profit than any quality of mercy. As he writes in "Demons One and All," "At the bar of justice/ Innocence is no bar to/ Conviction / Confinement / Condemnation / Consignment / To the junkyard of lost souls."

Not escaping Johnson's eye are the diverse inhabitants of this almost-forgotten place, both inmates and officers. He shows us all to be all too real. One cannot help feeling sympathy for the officers in the "Last Supper' who escort a condemned man to his death. They are condemned as well through their complicity, these "guests at a living wake." The execution is conducted with bureaucratic punctiliousness, but the officers go home afterwards emptied, craving the temporary amnesia of sleep. Not only prisoners are scarred by their time behind high walls and barbed wire.

In a few of these poems are echoes of the laughter, however bitter, that helps us cope with our time. Our laughter is not that of the oblivious or unrepentant. It stems from the black comedy of our existence. If we couldn't laugh, we would only weep. How then can we not smile grimly at the pathetic machinations of the predator in "Fishing," who uses as bait the only temptations he has left? That tragedy plays out in prison every day. All inmates know that loneliness is a powerful goad. One step in either direction could turn any of us into predator or prey. There are times when reducing such choices to the absurd is the only way to keep them from becoming irresistible.

Robert Johnson's poetry is neither frivolous nor self-serving. Poetry of witness rarely is. Instead, it offers stark testimony "of dreams gone sour/ of life died by the hour/ of death by decree/ Until you're set free / In this life or the next." Each poem compels its readers to hear Johnson's voice, as well as the voices of those who too often remain unheard. I hope they listen closely.

Erin George, #314542
Fluvanna Correctional Center for Women
Troy, Virginia
May 7, 2007

Afterword

In *Burnt Offerings*, Robert Johnson has opened a window onto an alien, forbidding landscape that is as far from the world the rest of us inhabit as Poe's "El Dorado." We are brought into the world of concertina wire and steel, the world of broken men and women longing for human touch and kindness with such power that we are forced to see and feel what Americans have chosen to ignore far too long: we are warehousing humans behind those walls. This collection addresses the myriad problems facing America's prisons and has the distinct advantage of simultaneously reaching diverse audiences, from academics with professional interest in the criminal justice system to the millions of men and women living in the often Kafkaesque environment Johnson describes.

In this volume, Johnson often asks the tough questions, as in "No Convict Left Behind," when he says, "We don't leave students behind/ no matter how troubled they may be/ Why abandon convicts?" Johnson brings to the forefront the realization that "A warehouse is no house of change." We are reminded that sending humans into the dungeon never to be heard from again is barbaric, and Johnson suggests that "prison could be a place of reflection." It is often just that for the men and women housed there, but the system refuses to honor the accomplishments of those held within its walls.

Johnson shows us the impact of life on death row in "Years of living alone" when he reminds us that "she" is but a fragment of her former self, "she paced daily, nightly, ever so lightly/ so as not to draw attention to herself/ what was left of her self/ barely visible/ behind the bars." This image burns indelibly on the brain and reminds us of the fragility of the human psyche and the power of the system to destroy.

Included are poems by two of Johnson's former students, Seri P. Irazola and Ania Dobrzanska, and a current student, Thaïs Miller. Johnson collaborated with one of them (Dobrzanska) on the poem "Cell Mate," a startling piece describing a predatory relationship and, like Eliot's *Waste Land*, hinting in the title's two-word construction of things unexpected: "Words that bite, tear my flesh" and a narrator who describes someone "feeding off my pain." Irazola paints word pictures in "Days of our lives" that show the reader how time stops behind the walls, and

Dobrzanska in "Solitary Soliloquy" offers that "It is me against the world and I am not/ ready." The remote world of the juvenile prisoner is the subject of Miller's poem, "The First Time I Saw That Place," a work marked by subtle understatement of the profound separation of imprisoned children from a society that has all but forgotten them. For prisoners locked away from all that is real, these losses are too often felt with every waking breath.

The poems in this collection take the reader on a walking tour through the darkest corridors of the bowels of America's prisons showing us places that invoke fear and sadness, inhumanity and horror, and we are reminded in words that evoke images of pain and loneliness, and often death, as in "SHU Fly" and "Face it," that to be incarcerated is a solitary existence.

Robert Johnson has brought the reader as close to incarceration as possible with his startling look at the realities of life behind bars. America has spent the last forty years building prisons with wild abandon and little regard to the consequences that mass incarceration has on society or the people it houses behind the bars and razor wire. In this rush to imprison, Johnson's portrait of the prison world we have wrought, as disturbing as it certainly is, must be examined if we are to alter the course of the mutually destructive path we have set for ourselves, even if we must look as Poe urged, "Over the mountains of the moon/ Down the valley of the shadow."° This Robert Johnson has done with style and power. *Burnt Offerings* will not be forgotten.

Susan Nagelsen
Professor of Writing
New England College
May 6, 2007

° Poe, Edgar Allen. "El Dorado"

About the Author

Robert Johnson is the author of *Poetic Justice: Reflections on the Big House, the Death House, and the American Way of Justice*, winner of the L.I.F.E. Award from WilloTrees Press. His poems have appeared in *Black Bear Review, The American Review, The National Catholic Reporter, Carnelian, CMC* (Crime Media Culture), *Dan River Anthology, Pleasant Living Magazine*, and *Tacenda Literary Magazine*. His short story, "The Practice of Killing," won the Wild Violet Fiction Contest for 2003. His first play, "Wheel of Torture," was published in *CMC* (Crime Media Culture). Other works of fiction include *Justice Follies: Parody from Planet Prison* and *The Crying Wall*, which he edited with Victor Hassine, a life-sentence inmate and Ania Dobrzanska. Johnson's best known work of social science, *Death Work: A Study of the Modern Execution Process*, won the Outstanding Book Award of the Academy of Criminal Justice Sciences.

About the Contributors

Ania Dobrzanska holds a B.A. in Psychology and Administration of Justice from Rutgers University and an M.S. in Justice, Law & Society from American University. She is a Certified Corrections Manager, a designation conferred by the American Correctional Association. Dobrzanska has published several articles in *Corrections Today* on issues of professionalism in corrections and leadership. She is co-author of a chapter on the history of prisons in *Prisons: Today and Tomorrow*, a widely used text; and co-author of an article on the adjustment of life-sentence prisoners published in *Corrections Compendium*, a peer-reviewed journal. Dobrzanska is also a published writer of fiction. Her short story, "Dances with Dragons: Memories of the Hole," appears in *The Crying Wall*, a book she co-edited.

Seri P. Irazola is a Research Associate I with the Urban Institute's Justice Policy Center. Dr. Irazola has more than five years of research experience in the fields of criminology and social policy. Her interests focus on inmate re-entry, recidivism, impact and conditions of incarceration, crime communities, violence, and victimization. Prior to joining the Justice Policy Center's team at the Urban Institute, Dr. Irazola was a Statistician for the Bureau of Justice Statistics, a branch of the U.S. Department of Justice, Office of Justice Programs. She received her Doctorate and Masters from American University in Washington, DC, and her Bachelors from the University of Michigan.

Thaïs H. Miller is an undergraduate student at American University majoring in Literature and minoring in Music Performance. Miller is an accomplished musician (violin) and a budding playwright. Her play, "The Price is Wrong: A Play in One Act with Vignettes," will appear in the 2008 issue of *Tacenda Literary Magazine*. After completing her undergraduate degree, Miller hopes to pursue her Master of Fine Arts in Creative Writing.

Susan Nagelsen is a Professor of Writing at New England College in Henniker, NH. She is an Associate Editor of the *Journal of Prisoners on Prison* and Editor of *Exiled Voices: Portals of Discovery* (Nov., 2007), an anthology of writing by imprisoned writers.

About the Artists

Jennifer Adger (Cover Art) is an award-winning artist whose work can be found in private collections in Alabama, California, the District of Columbia, Massachusetts, New York, and Virginia. Some of her work can be seen at www.jenniferadger.net/. Adger received her Bachelors Degree in Psychology from Auburn University and a Masters in Public Policy, with a concentration in Criminal Justice Policy, from the Kennedy School of Government at Harvard University. She is a doctoral candidate in Justice, Law and Society at American University.

Amy Hendrick (Cover Design) is an MFA candidate in American University's Film and Electronic Media Program. She has a background in youth development, graphic design, and photography.

Jason Diebler (Cover Design) has worked for the New Media Center at American University since 2004. He is an alumnus of American University, where he received his MFA in Film & Electronic Media from the School of Communication in 2006. His accomplishments in film and video include various film festival awards for his work as an editor, director, writer, and videographer.

CPSIA information can be obtained at www.ICGtesting.com
Printed in the USA
LVOW120357200412

278409LV00001B/14/A